DENIS HEALEY'S *Yorkshire Dales*

SAVE BEAUTIFUL YORKSHIRE

Annual Report

to the Friends of the Yorkshire Moor and Dales

"Thanks For Your Help"
A Message from Warden Bob Dicker

The Yorkshire Moors and Dales Appeal has meant a lot to me. My patch covers such diverse and splendid places as Roseberry Topping near Middlesbrough, Scarthwood Moor, Blakey Topping and Bridestones near Pickering.

Bob Dicker testing the purity of Staindale Beck through a detailed fish egg count.
NT\Fred Spencer

And the problems are just as varied as the countryside itself! Wildlife habitats under siege; drystone walls tumbling; footpaths worn out by the tramp of many feet. But with the help of the Appeal, we have been able to replant hedges with hawthorn, holly, field maple, blackthorn; pitch robust paths; replant oaks bordering our nature reserve; and monitor streams.

Footpath repair gang at work, Bridestones.
NT\Fred Spencer

I don't measure the Appeal's success in terms of how many yards of wall, hedge or footpath we've rebuilt. I measure it in the faces of our visitors. Like the older couple who told me that the repaired footpath on Bridestones meant they could now get back to a place they loved and thought they would never see again. And the school children who discovered a wonderful watery world in Staindale Beck and found out where the bluebells grow in Newton Wood. Then there are the future generations, because so much of our work is long term. We shall never witness their joy but I am sure it will be there.

But the hard truth is this. We can measure the outcome in smiles, but the income has to be in money.

Thank you for the help you have given me and my team out here on the North York Moors.
Please continue your support.

 THE NATIONAL TRUST

Facts and Figures

The Yorkshire Moors and Dales Appeal was launched in September 1991 and in its first twenty-four months raised £461,000 of which £189,000 came in during the last twelve months.

Friends	£211,000
Corporate and Sponsorship	£179,000
National Trust Centres	£39,000
Minster Concert	£17,000
Charitable Trusts	£9,000
Others	£6,000
Total	**£461,000**

The biggest contribution came from the Friends. Well over 3,000 generous donors who live not only in Yorkshire but throughout the country and abroad.

Corporate donors provided £179,000. British Coal Opencast has contributed towards moorland regeneration on Marsden Moor and rebuilding drystone walls. An important spin-off has been a technical exchange of views on methods of re-establishing heather and other moorland plant communities on eroded areas of National Trust moorland and reclaimed opencast sites. Yorkshire Electricity has generously

Grass of Parnassus - this delicate plant will thrive on the hillsides and valley bottoms of the Dales only if its habitat is protected.
D. Southall, Driffield

supported the Appeal at Hardcastle Crags. We arranged an on-pack promotion in 1992 with Taylors Tea and Coffee of Harrogate. Northumbrian Water made an important contribution in Cleveland and North Yorkshire. This year, Nordale Country Foods of Skipton who make traditional Yorkshire Puddings are helping the Appeal with an on-pack promotion in outlets such as Morrisons and Kwik-Save. A concert in York Minster sponsored by IBM raised £17,000. Centres and associations throughout the country again gave generously from their hard earned funds.

The Appeal will now be going flat out to reach the target of £750,000.

Two "Workhorses" join the team

Two refurbished Land Rovers have been given to the National Trust by corporate supporters Yorkshire Electricity and British Coal Opencast.

Hardcastle Crags Warden Keith Robinson got the keys of the ex Yorkshire Electricity "workhorse". Now it will support footpath repair work already aided by Yorkshire Electricity. Keith said that footpath repairs were making excellent progress "the Land Rover will help us keep moving forward".

Warden Keith Robinson and Forester Tim Lamb with the "Yorkshire Electricity" Land Rover.
Jack Hickes/Yorkshire Electricity.

The ex-British Coal Opencast "workhorse" was last used two hundred feet under ground on a South Wales opencast site. Now it is at work "on top of the world" along the cliff tops of North Yorkshire and Cleveland. Coastal Warden Richard Hodgson said "We can now get people and materials to some of the most remote and rugged stretches of the East Coast where the high moors meet the sea".

The two gifts bring big savings for the National Trust - now even more funds can go directly to conservation.

Warden Richard Hodgson in the driving seat of the "British Coal Opencast" Landrover with the Training forWork team fencing near Robin Hood's Bay.
Bill Devey/British

THE NATI

Handing on the Skills

Les Topham and Ian Guest have put their drystone walling skills together over many years and many miles. They each developed their techniques through training and working with the National Trust. Good foundations, secure "throughs" to give lateral strength, tight coping to bind the walls together, - skills acquired that will give long life to any wall they built.

Les Topham and Ian Guest at work, Bay Ness.
Bill Devey/British Coal Opencast

There are literally thousands of miles of drystone walls in the Yorkshire uplands. They not only provide efficient stock-proof boundaries to the fields, they also lend a very special quality to our Yorkshire landscape. Sadly, many of them are in dire need of repair. Without them, our hillsides would be bare and bland indeed.

Here at Bay Ness, north of Robin Hood's Bay this fine sandstone wall sits close to the well used Cleveland Way long distance footpath. It costs on average £15 to rebuild a yard of drystone wall and in 1993 the Appeal adopted a number of walls including this one at Bay Ness.

Les Topham says training is vital, we should not only hand on well built walls to future generations, but also the skill to keep them upright.

High Thorn Haw Barn Saved

High Thorn Haw Barn, perched above Beckermonds at the head of lonely Langstrothdale, has served for many, many years as a sturdy shelter for overwintering cattle. Not far from the Dalesway footpath and the upland route from Beckermonds to Littondale, it stands boldly in the wild and open landscape. After so many years in the harsh weather conditions of the dale, the heavy stone slab roof shifted bodily and the east gable bowed ominously. Without immediate attention this typical vernacular building was in danger of collapse. The repair team began work on the barn and their worst fears were confirmed. Without the roof to bind the walls together, the east gable simply fell down.

Now, re-using traditional materials, High Thorn Haw Barn has been saved. There are at least one hundred barns in Upper Wharfedale most of them requiring urgent repairs. A continuing task for the Yorkshire Moors and Dales Appeal.

Roof timbers exposed.   *Basil Brown*

Rebuilding the east gable.   *Basil Brown*

High Thorn Haw Barn and Beckermonds.   *Andy Tryner/National Trust*

Congratulations!

Lord Healey made Yorkshire Man of the Year

Appeal President Lord Healey of Riddlesden has been made Yorkshire Man of the Year 1993 for his leadership of the Yorkshire Moors and Dales Appeal and for his contribution to the county over many years.

The vital importance of the Appeal was well recognised by the Yorkshire Awards Committee. Lord Healey said he was delighted that the contribution of the Appeal to the county had been so fully appreciated.

Lord Healey was brought up in Keighley, attended Bradford Grammar School and represented Leeds East. He became President of the Appeal on 16 September 1991.

Previous winners of the Award have been Sir Jimmy Savile, heart surgeon Duncan Walker, Rt Hon Merlyn Rees and athlete Peter Elliott.

Lord Healey, Yorkshire Moors and Dales Appeal, Yorkshire Man of the Year 1993
NT/Simon Warner

Great Red Dome Rises Over Malham Tarn

An inch by inch fingertip survey of Tarn Moss alongside Malham Tarn has brought good news for Head Warden/Naturalist Alister Clunas. A National Vegetation Classification Survey revealed that the red sphagnum moss, *Sphagnum magellanicum*, on the raised bog was on the increase. This is the cheering outcome of a painstaking programme of care begun by Alister in 1987. The red sphagnum is one of the bog's main building blocks. Raised bogs are amongst Britain's rarer habitats, depending entirely on rainwater to keep them active. Rainwater is absorbed into the spongy moss, becomes acidic and slows down the decay of old vegetation. New growth springs up on top and the bog slowly rises above the surrounding levels.

In the past an attempt was made to drain the bog through "gripping", that is, digging deep drainage channels. With the help of volunteers, Alister blocked the drains and now his foresight is being amply rewarded. The red sphagnum domes with their copious water holding capacity are rising again. Insects flourish on the rain fed bog. In last year's Annual Report we noted the appearance of the large skipper butterfly and common darter dragonfly over Tarn Moss. Now we know why their rich variety is returning. The great red domes of Tarn Moss are growing again. Alister said that the Yorkshire Moors and Dales Appeal had helped to protect and restore scarce habitats like Tarn Moss but warned "there are still many more under threat".

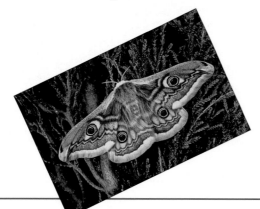

Emperor Moth (female).
N Harwood.

Produced with the support of

Yorkshire on Sunday

President of the Appeal: Lord Healey of Riddlesden
Appeal Manager: Adrian Alderson, Yorkshire Moors and Dales Appeal, The National Trust, Goddards, 27 Tadcaster Road, York YO2 2QG. Telephone: (0904) 702021
Design & Artwork: Dave Collier Graphics, York (0904) 641738   *The National Trust is a Registered Charity No. 205846*

Denis Healey (signature)

DENIS HEALEY'S *Yorkshire Dales*

A celebration of the Yorkshire Dales landscape

First published in Great Britain 1995 in hardback by
Dalesman Publishing Company Limited,
Stable Courtyard,
Broughton Hall,
Skipton,
North Yorkshire BD23 3AE

Published in paperback 1997
Reprinted in 1998

Text © 1995 Denis Healey, John Morrison, Colin Raw, Norman Duerden,
Maurice Colbeck
Photographs © Denis Healey, John Morrison, Colin Raw, Geoff Lund,
Norman Duerden

A British Library Cataloguing in Publication record is available for this book

ISBN 1 85568 097 1 (hardback)
ISBN 1 85568 135 8 (paperback)

Designed by Jonathan Newdick
Typeset by Southern Positives and Negatives (SPAN), Lingfield, Surrey
Colour origination by Primary Colour Ltd., London W4
Printed by Midas Printing Ltd., Hong Kong

PAGE TWO The hostile environment
surrounding reclaimed pastureland
near Garsdale Head with Wild Boar
Fell dominating the skyline.
Photograph by Colin Raw.

Contents

Burnsall, in Wharfedale.

My Yorkshire Dales

Often rebuked, yet always back returning
To those first feelings that were born with me,
And leaving busy chase of wealth and learning
For idle dreams of things which cannot be,

I'll walk where my own nature would be leading;
It vexes me to choose another guide;
Where the grey flocks in ferny glens are feeding,
Where the wild wind blows on the mountain side.

Emily Brontë speaks for me ever more urgently as I grow older. As a boy in Riddlesden on the slopes of Ilkley Moor, I looked across industrial Keighley to the village of Haworth, where Emily and her sisters distilled the essence of Yorkshire – half Irish like myself.

On Saturday afternoons and Sundays I explored every beck and crag on the moors above us; I built dams with stones and tussocks of grass, and forced my body into rocky caves in the hope of finding hidden treasure. Our favourite walk took us over the moors through Keighley Gate to the escarpment which overlooks Wharfedale from Bolton Abbey to Otley, past the prehistoric Swastika Stone to Windgate Nick. Then we went over the moors again, with a break to climb the Doubler Stones, and had tea at a farmhouse on paper-thin bread and butter with strawberry jam, before the last lap under Rivock Edge down to Riddlesden. In front of us lay Airedale, from the Druids' Altar above Bingley to the Pennine boundary between Yorkshire and Lancashire which stretched in a great arc on the horizon from Oxenhope to Malham.

I was only five years old when my father took me to Malham Cove and Gordale Scar, my little brother on his shoulders, to marvel at the limestone cliffs which had attracted England's greatest poets and painters for more than a hundred years. At that age I was less excited by the wrinkled white wall of the cove than by the black streak on its surface, which my father told me marked the descent of Tom, the chimney sweep in *The Water Babies*.

For ten days every Whitsun, we had our summer camp in a field by the River Wharfe below Appletreewick, a hamlet which in 1610 produced a Lord Mayor of London in Sir William Craven. A century later the lovely village of Linton produced another Yorkshire Whittington, Richard Fountaine, who also made his fortune in London.

Such historical accidents meant nothing to me in those days; it was their natural perfection which attracted me to the Dales. Each season has its special beauty – summer when the bracken is green and sweet to smell, autumn when it is golden brown and the moors are flooded with purple heather, winter when all is white with snow and an icy wind makes your eyes water. But loveliest of all is spring, when primroses stud the grey stone walls, the lush meadows are sprinkled with cowslips, and pools of bluebells glow luminous in the woods. And above all this the larks rising and falling in the pure sky: 'It was all Adam and maiden, and fire, green as grass.'

Our favourite walk from camp was through the fields by the river to Barden Bridge, built by Lady Anne Clifford below her castle after the Civil War. Then we scrambled through the beautiful woods by the Strid to Bolton Abbey – to me the loveliest of all medieval ruins. After eating our sandwiches on the grassy bank opposite the Abbey while chaffinches fought over the crumbs, we would climb up the Valley of Desolation with its silvery waterfall, over the moors to the crags of Simon's Seat, and then race headlong down through the woods and fields and back to camp. The area has been irresistibly attractive to artists with brush and pen, from Wordsworth and Turner to the 'silent' traveller from China, Chiang Yee, fifty years ago. John Ruskin celebrated its beauty unforgettably in *Modern Painters*:

> Up the valley the limestone summits rise, and that steeply, to a height of 1,200 feet above the river which foams between them in the narrow and dangerous channel of the Strid. Noble moorlands extend above, purple with heath, and broken into scars and glens; and around every soft tuft of wood, and gentle extent of meadow, throughout the dale, there floats a feeling of this mountain power and an instinctive apprehension of the strength and greatness of the wild northern land. It is to the association of this power and border sternness with the sweet peace and tender decay of Bolton Priory, that the scene owes its distinctive charm.

In my later years at school I would spend my weekends exploring the upper Dales on foot and bicycle, staying at youth hostels or farmhouses. My favourite ride was over the grass carpet of Mastiles Lane from Grassington to Malham. The streams at the head of Wharfedale flowed past particularly attractive villages – Arncliffe in Littondale, and Starbotton and Buckden beyond Kettlewell, from which I would pedal panting up

Arncliffe, in Littondale.

through Cray and over to Aysgarth in Wensleydale with its lovely falls.

During the war, before I went to North Africa, I did my courting in Wharfedale, so when Edna and I got married just before Christmas 1945, it was to Wharfedale I looked for our honeymoon. The only place I could find was the Buck Inn at Buckden. It was still crowded with middle-aged ladies from the nearby industrial towns seeking refuge from the war, so we had to sleep in the loft of the barn next door. As soon as we got into bed a trapdoor in the floor would open and a head would appear, followed by a body holding a candle. It was the owner of the barn, a little old lady who wrote poetry and wanted us to hear her works.

If she expected to interrupt us in some amorous exercises she must have been disappointed. I had developed a painful boil at the base of my spine, and Edna spent most of our honeymoon bathing it. I did, however, give the other guests a certain thrill one morning when I walked into breakfast with the words: 'Christ, my coccyx is painful today!' I suspect their knowledge of anatomy was no match for their imaginations.

In the forty-five years that followed, politics limited my opportunities to re-visit the Dales, though with a constituency in Leeds I did manage the odd afternoon at Bolton Abbey.

But something was changing. By the 1950s the end of the petrol rationing and the post-war rise in prosperity meant that roads which were almost empty when I had travelled on them on my bicycle were now choked by cars inching forward bumper to bumper, the stench of their petrol fouling the scented air. The difficulty of making a living by grazing sheep on the stony hillsides was driving men off the farms into the nearby towns. Away from roads, on the paths by the rivers or over the moors, the countryside was as beautiful as ever; but the dry-stone walls were crumbling, the empty barns were beginning to lose their roofs, and even their walls, and the more popular walks were wearing away. So when, in 1991, after deciding to leave the House of Commons, I was asked by Jennifer Jenkins if I could preside over the National Trust's Appeal for the Yorkshire Moors and Dales, I jumped at the chance. In the last four years I have been able to refresh my love for my old haunts in Airedale and Wharfedale, and to enjoy the beauties of other dales, as well as seeing for the first time the North York Moors from Bridestones to Roseberry Topping, and revisiting my childhood playground of Hardcastle Crags on the edge of the Brontë country.

I launched my appeal at Yockenthwaite, in the most inauspicious circumstances – a September day when heavy rain and dense mist made the hillsides invisible. Edna and I had spent the previous night at our beloved Red Lion Hotel in Burnsall. It had been arranged that we would descend next morning like heavenly messengers from high in the sky in a helicopter. In fact we had to fly up the narrowing valley at treetop height, hoping that the pilot would have time to avoid the higher branches as they loomed out of the fog in front of us. He did. Then I had to stumble about on the stones in the middle of the swollen infant river in borrowed wellingtons while the press took innumerable photo-

Yockenthwaite, where the National Trust's Appeal for the Yorkshire Moors and Dales was launched.

graphs, hoping to catch me crashing ingloriously into the stream. I survived the ordeal, and was rewarded by a long conversation with Graham Watson who had just given that enchanting tract of Upper Wharfedale to the Trust. He was a hale and hearty young man of eighty-two with a handsome, clean-shaven, ruddy face. His passion was riding his motorbike at eighty miles an hour; he had just made a journey from Bradford to Cambridge and back in a single day. He was part-owner of Lister's Mills, and his father had given John Christie the velvet for his new opera house at Glyndebourne in the thirties.

Graham Watson was typical of the public-spirited Yorkshiremen whom I was to meet during the following years. Even more impressive were the tenant farmers whose care for the environment was to make the Trust's conservation work possible. After some years in Saudi Arabia, showing the Arabs how to raise cattle, Chris Akrigg was bringing up a young family on a hill farm at Cray, above Buckden; one winter he and his wife had sewn tough strips of cloth over the nether regions of more than a hundred ewes as a primitive form of birth control.

Meeting farmers like this, and the patient craftsmen who led teams of unemployed lads from the Yorkshire towns and cities in rebuilding the dry-stone walls and collapsing barns, gave me a new insight into the Dales as the homeland of living communities with their roots deep in the past.

Mr Umpelby from Newhouse Farm, Malham, a typical Dales farmer.

The names of their villages testify to the waves of invaders, successively from central Europe, Rome, Normandy, and the Nordic countries who had established settlements over the thousand years before the end of the Middle Ages. It was easier now for me to believe what a Norwegian friend had once told me: 'If we'd had another hundred men in the Battle of Stamford Bridge the whole world would now be talking Norwegian!' It was said that in 1940, when some of the dalesmen landed in Norway, they had little difficulty in understanding the language.

The Celts left behind relics of their pagan rituals, like the Swastika Stone above Ilkley. The Romans left roads and some impressive ruins. The Scandinavians left place names and some of their vocabulary. The most lasting impact was made by the Normans. The abbeys and monasteries they founded survived four centuries until Henry VIII dissolved them, as much to get hold of their riches as to defy the Pope who opposed his divorce.

By the middle of the 15th century the religious orders had transformed the economy of the Yorkshire Dales and had become immensely wealthy in the process. Fountains Abbey, between the entrances to Nidderdale and Wensleydale, had been founded in 1132 by a small group of monks in York who felt that the Benedictine Order, to which they belonged, was straying from its vows of poverty, so they established a Cistercian settlement in 'the waste howling wilderness' of Skelldale. They began raising sheep simply to provide wool for their clothes. Before long gifts of land were flowing in to them from wealthy noblemen who hoped thereby to purchase their passports to heaven.

So the monks of Fountains Abbey ended up owning more than a million acres all over the Dales; they became the leading sheep farmers in Britain, producing an annual output of nearly 28,000 lbs of the finest wool, much of which they exported as far away as Flanders and Florence. They used to drive their flocks from Malham to Kilnsey along my favourite bicycle run, Mastiles Lane. Wool was by now the largest single contributor to the nation's wealth – which is why I watch the Lord

Kilnsey Crag, one of the best-known and most photographed sights in Wharfedale.

Chancellor presiding over the House of Lords from the Woolsack. After the Dissolution, the Dales went on producing wool from private farms and it was scoured, carded, combed and spun in the villages. The knitting of socks and caps became a major industry all over the Dales.

The Cistercian monks were also responsible for turning lead mining into a major industry, starting with Jervaulx Abbey, followed by Fountains and Byland. After the Dissolution prospecting for lead was often carried out by farmers, mainly in Swaledale and Arkengarthdale, and from Nidderdale over to Wharfedale – particularly on the moors between Grassington and Pateley Bridge. And there was some mining for coal. When I was a boy in Riddlesden the moor grass below Rivock Edge was pock-marked with what we called pot holes – shallow but steep depressions from which they had once extracted surface coal. As children we competed to push one another down them during our walks; later they allowed us to cuddle our girlfriends without fear of discovery.

Burnsall, a small community but with a favourite hotel.

There was even a tiny coal mine still in operation, with a shaft about thirty feet deep and four feet wide, from which two old men still managed to scratch a living.

Nowadays the derelict ruins left by the lead mines, and the moor-sides they defaced, are cherished as archaeological monuments to an industry which helped to provide roofs for our medieval castles and churches. We are far less tolerant of 20th-century quarries and power lines. Studley Royal appears to us now as a gem of 18th-century landscape gardening. But when it was built by the disgraced Chancellor of the Exchequer, John Aislabie, he was attacked by William Gilpin, prophet of the picturesque, for 'a vain ostentation of expense, . . . decorated in a taste debauched in its conception, and puerile in its execution.' The dry-stone walls which give the Dales their special character today did not exist at that time; they were mainly the product of the Enclosure Act of 1801.

The never-ending interaction between nature and man has given the Dales a special beauty which it is our duty to protect, even though that will sometimes mean changing the traditional function of ancient buildings. Malham Tarn House, in the woods on the northern shore of Malham Tarn is an example. The present building was erected in the 18th century on the foundations of a much older house as a shooting lodge for James Lister of Gisburn, who became the first Lord Ribblesdale. In the second half of the 19th century Walter Morrison, a wealthy Liberal from Eton and Balliol, made it a refuge for eminent Victorians such as Charles Darwin, John Stuart Mill, John Ruskin and the authors of *Tom Brown's Schooldays* and *The Water Babies*. Indeed the latter, Charles Kingsley, included a superb description of the landscape there as 'Vendale' in his book. Now it is owned by the National Trust and used by the Field Studies Council as a centre for studying the local flora and fauna. The nearby nature reserve is under the direction of a botanist from the Orkneys, National Trust head warden, Alister Clunas. There is a cunning hide at the water's edge where visitors can watch and photograph an astonishing variety of birdlife.

With the decline of hill farming and the adoption of new techniques for farming, more and more barns and cottages are being converted for holiday use by invaders from the industrial cities nearby. This has often improved the beauty of the villages, which now enjoy a profusion of flowers unknown in my childhood. One of my best friends in Leeds bought a house in the exquisite old village of West Burton in Wensleydale, where, as an MP, I used to visit her. Though by profession a speculative builder, she became a passionate conservationist! Those who see weekenders as foreigners with no right to a home in the Dales should remember that the Norman monasteries of which we are now so proud were much more foreign when they were first set up.

Television has made the Dales familiar to millions all over the world who previously had no conception of their beauty. *Emmerdale Farm* offers an amalgam of many Yorkshire scenes and characters, while *All Creatures Great and Small* was shot mainly in Swaledale, Coverdale and Wensleydale. So I knew Swaledale long before I first went there in 1984; but I must accept that its upper reaches, from Gunnerside to Keld, are as beautiful as anything more familiar to me. Presumably television has not yet discovered Bransdale, a hidden valley in the moors, a Yorkshire Shangri-La accessible only to those with a Ph.D in map reading.

I have recently been able to use television myself to convey my love for the Dales, discovering new beauties in the process. In making a programme on Bolton Abbey in the cold Easter of 1993, when the icy

Bolton Abbey, the setting for an Augustinian priory and now for an Anglican church.

wind almost froze the young daffodils in the cemetery, I discovered that there was the pagan figure of the Green Man among the decorations on the roof, while the Augustinian priory is now an Anglican church – a monument to the universality of the spirit. Unfortunately the worn stepping-stones across the Wharfe I had known as a child have been replaced with substitutes which are under water except in summertime.

A few months later I was interviewed by Harry Secombe in a howling gale near a barn above Kettlewell. To the astonishment of the camera crew we kept warm by singing Neapolitan songs we had learned in the war when we both served in Italy.

I frequently return to the Gothic majesty of Fountains Abbey, which also boasts a Green Man. One summer evening the National Trust held a concert on the wide lawns in front of the ruins; an orchestra played 19th-century French operetta while the audience of thousands, many in Edwardian costume, concluded the proceedings by dancing the cancan, Edna and I among them. There is no better way to celebrate the joy of living, even in a monastery garden.

I have learned in the last few years that the key to the success of the National Trust in preserving this part of Britain's landscape is its inalienable ownership of the land and buildings for which it is responsible, and the commitment of the wardens, land agents and farmers who look after them on the ground. These men and women combine Wordsworth's deep love for the countryside with the tough pragmatism of

Drebley, in Wharfedale.

DENIS HEALEY'S YORKSHIRE DALES

Tennyson's Northern Farmer. They form a community as dedicated as that which looked after the monasteries so many centuries ago. It has been a privilege for me to know them as friends.

Reconciling preservation with improved access presents difficult dilemmas. Change is as inevitable in the future as it has been in the past. In medieval times the bodies of the dead were carried down Corpse Way from Upper Swaledale in wicker coffins on the backs of dalesmen, to be buried in consecrated ground at Grinton – the nearest parish church. No one would now forbid the use of a hearse out of respect for that tradition.

But there are new threats to the Dales, as to other parts of the countryside, from the imminent collapse of the Common Agricultural Policy, which has already created wildernesses through the practice of 'set-aside'. The horrific increase in motor traffic and the privatisation of water will also have catastrophic effects unless their consequences are far more carefully considered and controlled.

This book demonstrates in its pictures better than any argument why it is worth spending time and money to preserve the beauty of the Yorkshire Dales against these threats. The case is summed up in the final verse of Emily Brontë's poem:

What have those lonely mountains worth revealing?
More glory and more grief than I can tell.
The earth that wakes one human heart to feeling
Can centre both the worlds of heaven and hell.

LORD HEALEY OF RIDDLESDEN, 1995

*Lord Healey, who took the photographs which accompany this Intro-
duction, is President of the Yorkshire Moors and Dales Appeal.*

A sheep is silhouetted in the arched
doorway of a typical Wensleydale
field-barn near Hawes.

Architecture without architects

JOHN MORRISON

The Yorkshire Dales, far from being wilderness, comprise a managed landscape, where the hand of man is everywhere in evidence. In the dry-stone walls that snake their way up vertiginous fells. In the barns that, in some parts, seem to occupy a corner of every field. In the packhorse bridges that span the becks. In the wayside chapels: as solid and uncompromising as the faith that built them. In the mines and mills that created work for those who did not farm. In the villages, whose houses huddle together as if to shield themselves from wind and weather.

The vernacular buildings of the Yorkshire Dales present a beguiling picture of an architecture without architects: buildings whose style seems to harmonise simply and unselfconsciously with the landscape they occupy. Lovers of stately homes will have to look elsewhere, for the buildings of the Yorkshire Dales are modest and unpretentious.

Nothing, it seems, was done for mere show, which is one reason why the villages still look 'of a piece'. Another is that, despite a recent trend towards buying Dales cottages as holiday retreats and retirement homes, the Dales population has continued to decline since early Victorian times. Thousands of men made a living – albeit a precarious one – from lead mining. The scars remain on the landscape, but the miners are gone. The smelt-mills were ransacked for their dressed stone, which, depending on your viewpoint, was either creative recycling or architectural vandalism.

Certainly the urge to preserve buildings long after their usefulness has gone, belongs to a more recent – and prosperous – age. Debates about what should be done to conserve the stone walls and field barns will become ever more urgent as the buildings continue to fall into ruin.

The truth is that the barns and walls have been typical of the Dales landscape for less than three centuries. Indeed, many travellers who visited the area in the years following the Enclosure Acts were appalled by the dividing up of what had largely been open country. Further, it was no accident that the Acts favoured wealthy landowners, who could afford to surround their land with stone walls, rather than the subsistence farmers who could not.

The Dales landscape has always been in flux. It may be unfeasible to 'stop the clock' and ossify the landscape in the form in which we see it today. But the argument that the Dales landscape deserves our protection is pressing. I hope my own feelings are revealed through these pictures. My watchword during this project has been to reveal not merely what a place looked like but also what it felt like.

John Morrison is a freelance writer and photographer with more than twenty books to his credit. From his base in the Yorkshire town of Hebden Bridge he is handily placed to build his impressive collection of photographs on the theme of 'the life and landscape of the North of England'. Here he concentrates on the ancient and traditional architecture of the Dales, typified by the numerous stone field-barns and dry-stone walls.

Crackpot Hall, the house with surely
the most beautiful view in Swaledale.
Lead mining built it and, ironically,
it was lead mining subsidence that
eventually destroyed it.

Countersett: a tiny collection of
characterful buildings, overlooking
Semerwater, made more colourful by
a profusion of wild flowers.

Haymaking time: this was the view
from my back door when I lived briefly
in the Wensleydale village of West
Witton.

The Georgian facades of Frenchgate
sweep down towards the huge market
square in Richmond.

Just before a storm – or just afterwards – the light can be remarkable; getting soaked seems a small price to pay for a picture. This is Dent preparing for a deluge.

Penyghent, one of the famous Three Peaks, emerging from the morning mist. Mist can change the landscape dramatically, making even familiar landmarks seem mysterious.

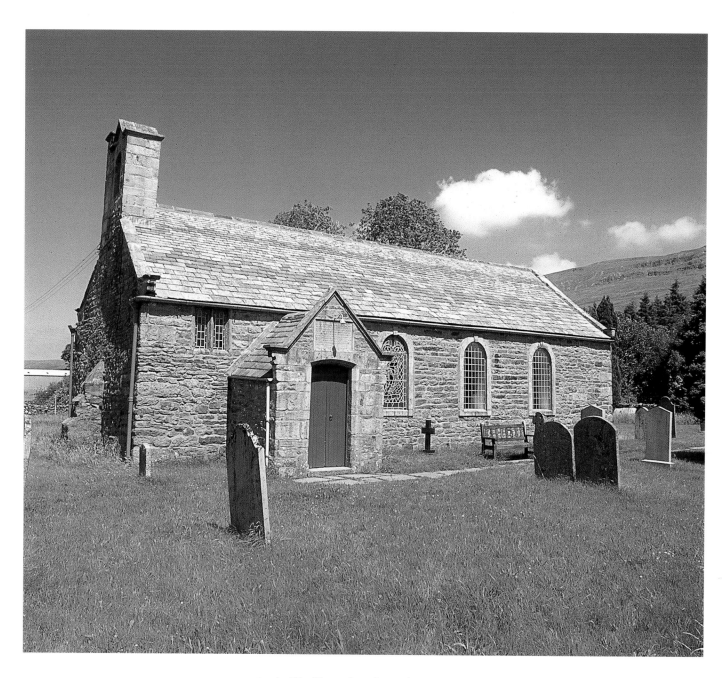

Outhgill village church, in the
Mallerstang valley. The inscribed
plaque over the doorway recalls that
this was one of the many buildings
restored by the redoubtable Lady
Anne Clifford.

Lady Anne Clifford's remarkable
almshouses, the hospital near
Beamsley: one of my favourite
buildings in the Dales.

Frenchgate, and the square keep of Richmond Castle, emerging from a blanket of mist. When lighting conditions are so odd, you have to shoot a lot of film, bracket exposures, and hope for the best.

There are no longer any markets in Askrigg, but this old, stepped market cross provides a tangible link with the past.

Low evening light brings a peach-coloured glow to a farmhouse in Burtersett, a little village near Hawes in Wensleydale.

Bealer Bank, a paved causeway built to allow the people of Gayle to walk dry-shod to their devotions at Hawes Church, through this pleasing wall-stile.

A colourful corner of Thornton Rust,
with garden flowers making a dramatic
contrast to the grey, rough-hewn
stonework so typical of vernacular
buildings in the Dales.

Brigflatts Quaker Meeting House, just
outside Sedbergh: a haven of silence,
a modest building of great charm and
the oldest meeting house in the North
of England.

I am intrigued by the date-stones over the doorways of so many Dales buildings. This example, in Hawes, offers the date, the initials of the original owner . . . and an 'improving' message to boot.

Dent has the confusing distinction of lying both in Cumbria and within the Yorkshire Dales National Park. With its cobbled streets and white-washed houses, it's a delightful spot.

The field-barns of the southern dales
– this one is near Malham – tend to be
larger and more elaborate in design
than those in Swaledale.

A track between fields near Aysgarth in Wensleydale. I don't know of any vernacular buildings that suit their surroundings as completely as the field-barns of the Dales.

High summer in West Witton:
Wensleydale hay in the fields, a
flowery path leading down to the
River Ure and an obliging seagull.

A fascinating corner of Wharfedale:
just outside Grassington. Here is
Grass Wood (an ash wood on
limestone) a photogenic pattern
of walls and barns.

ARCHITECTURE WITHOUT ARCHITECTS

The remains of the Old Gang lead mining complex in Swaledale. Here, a century ago, hard-won galena was smelted in these remote furnaces.

Mist shrouds the flanks of Kisdon Hill. Swaledale barns tend to be of simple design: the template for those little houses on a Monopoly board . . .

Typical Wharfedale scenery, near Kettlewell: limestone walls, limestone barns and limestone scars on the hill-top.

Hurst was once a bustling village, whose prosperity was won through lead mining. It was too remote to survive when the industry died. Now Hurst comprises just a handful of farms and barns.

ARCHITECTURE WITHOUT ARCHITECTS

Whenever possible I like to keep my pictures simple. A pair of barns, the sinuous shapes of three dry-stone walls and a few grazing cows create an almost still-life near Burtersett, Wensleydale.

A shaft of sunlight illuminates the asymmetric tower of Hawes Church against the shadowed background of the Wensleydale fells.

Cottages – and the lake of a fish farm – beneath the distinctive 'beak' of Kilnsey Crag, one of Wharfedale's most familiar landmarks.

You have to follow in the steps of the old lead miners, almost to the head of Gunnerside Gill, Swaledale, to find the evocative ruins of Blakethwaite smelt-mill.

A laithe-house – combining dwelling and barn under one roofline – stands alone in the bleak yet beautiful Mallerstang valley.

DENIS HEALEY'S YORKSHIRE DALES

LEFT It's good to climb a nearby hill, in order to see a village in its context: you begin to see why communities grew where they did. This is Burnsall, by a bend in the River Wharfe.

Even the simplest of elements – a Swaledale barn, a track and a dry-stone wall – can make a picture. Landscape photography is as much about what you leave out of a picture as what you leave in.

A solitary farmstead in Arkengarthdale, a valley that went from boom to bust during the second half of the 19th century. The lead mines closed and mining families were forced to move away.

In summer the village green of
Arncliffe, Littondale, is transformed
into a wildflower meadow. Can there
be a more happily sited red telephone
box in the land?

Low-lying mist creates a surreal scene that could almost be a painted backdrop for some theatrical production. This is Upper Swaledale, near Thwaite: a landscape that never disappoints.

The village of West Tanfield backs onto the River Ure to create a scene that has adorned countless calendars and biscuit-tin lids.

A tiny, shepherd's hut is one of the few buildings to be found along the road between Hawes and Ribblehead.

A study in monochrome that reminds me of the winter paintings by Breughel. This is Langthwaite Church in Arkengarthdale.

Foxgloves at Hebden Gill. This would
have been a busier scene in the days of
lead mining when the main road to the
mines ran through.

The search for perfection

GEOFF LUND

The dual occupations of dry-stone waller and scenic photographer may seem incompatible to many minds but in fact they are not. Both demand the search for perfection and require that the craftsman is first and foremost a countryman.

As a lad, the son of a gamekeeper in Malhamdale, the walk to school was six miles through magnificent Dales scenery. This experience gave me an abiding love of the sights and sounds of the Dales. One treasured memory is of when I first saw an almost magical mist 'just sitting' over Malham.

It was National Service in the Far East which first introduced me to the camera. As an energetic young artilleryman in Hong Kong, there was the need to find something to pass the off-duty hours and prevent boredom. Photography seemed the answer. The multi-racial crowded streets of Hong Kong offered inexhaustible subjects for the camera; the Heights, superlative views. Briefly I experimented with video but for me it lacked the appeal of still photography.

The pastel tints of the Dales might have seemed insipid after the vivid colours of Hong Kong. Not to me. Here is where I belonged.

As for any artist, there are loves and hates. In photography I abhor straight lines. The loves include waterfalls, bridges, steam trains puffing along the Settle–Carlisle line, animals of all kinds and especially the sheep and cattle I encounter as I trek, laden with photographic gear, across the haunting, ever-changing Yorkshire Dales.

Geoff Lund is an extraordinary man who combines traditional dry-stone walling with high-class photography. He is able to carry heavy photographic equipment to places where others would not venture and his strength is such that he rarely uses a tripod to hold the camera steady. Brought up on the fells above Malham, he knows the Dales and their features better than most, and his photographs capture their ever-changing moods with the greatest of sympathy.

This is the stream on Coniston Moor.
On the right is where a group of pot-
holers tragically died in 1967.

Gorgeous autumn tints in the Valley of Desolation at Bolton Priory. I love to walk here. It's actually called Posforth Gill but has been known as the Valley of Desolation since a great storm last century.

Overlooking Park Rash – the children from this old farm at the top of Coverdale used to spend weekdays down in Kettlewell, going to school, and come back home at the weekends.

Beckermonds, where the River Wharfe begins. The bridge takes you to High and Low Greenfield. It's a pity the ducks didn't co-operate, but I'd no bread to tempt them with that day.

The old packhorse bridge in Linton. There's another old bridge, which the main road runs over, and a very narrow footbridge at this end which may have been built for horses and traps.

DENIS HEALEY'S YORKSHIRE DALES

I was walking across a field one day
when these sheep caught my eye.
They're not Dales sheep but a rare
breed called Woodland.

Mid-afternoon is the only time to
capture Gordale Scar waterfall with
sun on it. You have to walk along a
steep road of shale that is giving way
all the time. It's a sombre scene.

THE SEARCH FOR PERFECTION

The most photographed tree in Malhamdale. It always makes me think of Africa, in the way it's standing there against all the odds. It's growing out of a crevice in the limestone rock and is about sixty years old.

Flowers add a lovely splash of colour looking towards Loup Scar near Burnsall. Sadly, a tree has fallen and killed this scene since I took the photograph.

Long Ashes, looking towards
Grassington with Simon's Seat in
the far distance.

Popular Deepdale, where the beck weaves its way through several National Trust properties is a great tourist attraction. You go on to Beckermonds then Oughtershaw and Hawes. When I was younger a bus came this way, probably via Cray.

Buckden in autumn. The hill at the back is where the fell race is run. That's a beautiful limestone wall.

Malham Tarn, now owned by the National Trust, is near where I was born and where my dad was keeper in the 30s. There's the iciest wind I know coming across here in winter but in summer there's a lovely, cool breeze.

Thornton Force is a great tourist
attraction at the head of Ingleton Falls.
A farmer told me he'd found lots of
visitors there at 6.30 in the morning –
he said it was like Blackpool!

This is a sad autumn scene by the Wharfe between Grassington and Hebden. It's a long walk but I just had to capture that tree. It's a dead elm. There are hundreds like this one and it's amazing how they can stand for so long without leaves or bark.

DENIS HEALEY'S YORKSHIRE DALES

This is what remains of the old
drovers' road between Grassington
and Hebden, probably at least two
to three hundred years old.

The old miners' road at Hebden Gill.
There's a lovely walk over to
Yarnbury.

DENIS HEALEY'S YORKSHIRE DALES

Swinnergill in Swaledale. I toyed with
the idea of waiting for the cloud to
move but instead used it to give the
picture depth. Beside the marvellous
little bridge are the remains of the
washing plant of the old lead mine.

DENIS HEALEY'S YORKSHIRE DALES

There are not many perfect days at Gouthwaite Reservoir. I waited a long time to capture the ripples. The water is almost like ice.

Bolton Priory is one of my favourite places on a lovely summer's day. I particularly like the way the tree is balanced.

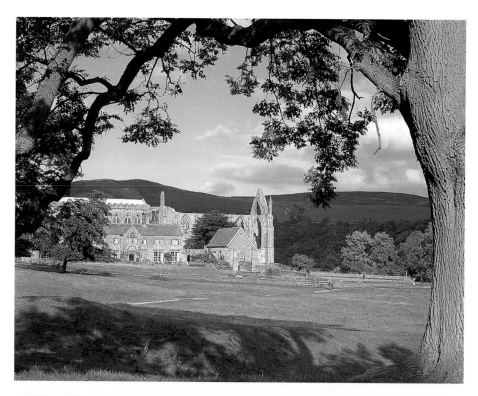

Dales photos often lend themselves to what I call 'basin' shots. Looking towards Burnsall, the River Wharfe is on the left and Appletreewick on the right. The yellow flowers are nicknamed 'dogstanders'.

A perfect day in the Wharfedale village
of Starbotton. The track at the back
goes up to a little water supply.

It's a tough walk up Ingleborough and
when all the elements attack you up
here it's really rough.

I was going from Starbotton to Buckden and I came across these icicles. An incredible number of people stopped here to photograph them.

This lovely winter scene was taken
from off the road between Hawes and
Oughtershaw. Hang-gliders take off in
the summer from the hilltop where I
was parked.

DENIS HEALEY'S YORKSHIRE DALES

I took this on a bitterly cold day between Hubberholme and Cray. I'd been past here many times before but not seen the tree. I was astounded by how many branches were running out from one big root.

Artengill in Dentdale. Sometimes you come across views like this by accident. Other times you have to hunt for them.

'Journey to Arcady'; an oystercatcher
returns to her eggs in the idyllic
setting of a beach in Littondale.

Paradise found

NORMAN DUERDEN

To the student of geology much of the appeal of the area between Ribble and Stainmore – the so-called Askrigg block – lies in its diversity of rock forms. Photographer and artist will enthuse over its dramatic topography, the scenic interplay of slate, limestone, grit and shales. With such a wealth of habitats it is hardly surprising that this countryside is attractive to the naturalist.

Each of its many manifestations – pavement, scarp, pothole, scree and outcrop – provides a new array of species particularly exciting to the newcomer. Half a century on, one remembers above all the initial impact of its austere beauty and its infinite photographic possibilities.

Its high places, discovered with satisfaction, were more frequented by waders – golden plover, lapwing, curlew and dunlin – than by humans. Foxes infrequently seen by day were revealed by an abundance of cat-like prints after overnight snow; badgers had frolicked on the fellside above Pateley Bridge.

Of the more aristocratic raptors, today the peregrine is celebrating a recovery; the moorland merlin, on the other hand, seems scarcely to hold its own. On a wild March day recently, the aerobatics of a rival buzzard and raven, sustained on the upward blast, gave Oxnop Scar a new dimension.

As there is a 'tide in the affairs of men' so too in the occurrences of the wild creatures of the Dales. One could mark a calendar and set down a route for their observation. Towards the end of March, for instance, oystercatchers will appear on the shingle above Gearstones; while along the Wharfe in April, those who linger by Barden Bridge can watch for the dipper feeding young below the parapet. In May the descent into Penyghent Gill is a dream: the cuckoo sings as if he had found paradise, and the country-lover may experience similar sentiments. Primroses bloom on into June: to them, in a hollow in a bank, sandpipers return year after year to nest. Their shrill, hysterical call echoes in the green confines of the gorge. Here, where water cascades over the steps of the Yoredale limestone, their companions are dipper and grey wagtail. Those observers who have the temerity to make the long scramble down the gill should be sure of their timing; May blossom, and the beloved bird's-eye primroses in bloom by the roadside below Penyghent, are reliable indicators.

Naturalist Norman Duerden took his first nature picture with an ancient brass and mahogany plate camera. More than twenty years later, using 35 mm equipment and working from a hide, he began colour photography of the wildlife around his home on the edge of the Yorkshire Dales. The results of Norman's patient efforts have appeared in his books on the Dales and been used in BBC broadcasts. Formerly a college principal, he spends his retirement in a small village above the River Ribble.

One swallow doesn't make a summer
– or so they say. But one sandpiper,
flickering along the surface of a hill
stream, certainly makes a spring – a
timely companion for primrose and
violet.

A snipe leads its chicks through the
water-meadows.

Golden plover chicks, hatched on exposed moorland, are dried off, and here tended by the female.

You may call him lapwing, plover, tewitt or peewit, according to your mood. His piercing cry and whirligig nuptial flight are features of a Dales spring.

A sitting curlew, apparently
unimpressed with her month-long
view of Penyghent, turns her eggs in
anticipation of the hatch.

The rare dotterel, aristocrat among the Scottish breeders, may appear briefly on the summits of the Dales on its journey north. The dotterel is almost indifferent to the presence of man.

A badger returns to its underground
sett in the roots of a dead tree.

The breathtaking swoop of the
hunting peregrine is one of the most
thrilling sights of nature; watch for it
over Dent and Ribblesdale.

Moorland tarns like those above
Swaledale are the breeding haunt
of the black-headed gull.

The name 'wood mouse' is hardly
appropriate for a creature which has
a range of habitats that includes
domestic and farm buildings.

The snoring of the hibernating
hedgehog may cause him to be
revealed to the prowling fox.

In the autumn serenity of a northern
river, a pensive heron stands
motionless.

Country lads called this the 'writing master' – a name suggested by the curiously scribbled eggshell of the yellowhammer.

A cock chaffinch at the nest.

The kingfisher's nesting chamber is excavated in a clay or sandy river bank.

Older naturalists remember the disappointment of nature photography in monochrome and greeted with acclaim the arrival of colour film. Even this pales when compared with the impact of the original experience.

The beauty of a May meadow, resplendent with flowers, is complemented by that of the attractive and successful orange-tip butterfly.

The moorhen eschews moors, but is a bird of pond, lake and backwater. It was originally the 'mere hen'.

No need to be apprehensive of the
harmless grass snake.

The pied wagtail occurs in numbers
along stretches of intake walling.

Sadness and sympathy are sentiments
one may feel for the brown hare, now
in decline, and with all hands raised
against him.

DENIS HEALEY'S YORKSHIRE DALES

Though more familiar as a resident of the Scottish Highlands, the mountain (or blue) hare is now found south of the border. In the Pennines the animal probably never attains the completely white pelage.

Young conifer plantations, with their abundance of voles, attract the diurnal short-eared owl, which often appears in numbers to nest.

Like its larger cousin the golden eagle, the buzzard is not averse to a meal of carrion.

The Howgills and adjacent valleys are
the headquarters of Dales buzzards.

Nobody's friend – a carrion crow at the nest.

In September, with the nesting season over, adult birds and young begin preparation for winter: rooks, jackdaws and pigeons flock together to gorge in the granary of the stubble field.

Fruit growers hate the bullfinch. I do not grow fruit. I love the bullfinch which sometimes nests in the garden.

Moss pools and moorland tarns attract
the redshank, winged watch-dog of
this damp Valhalla.

The apparent lifelessness and silence
of great conifer plantations, like those
in Widdale, are often relieved by the
needle-like notes of the goldcrest,
which hangs its tiny hammock
beneath a fir bough.

The robin is a strictly territorial bird and disputes over nest sites are common. Here, an ivy-covered wall provides suitable cover.

A human with half the qualities of the spotted flycatcher would be an admirable companion. Gentle and unassuming and guileless, it is equally at home in the intimacy of the cottage garden or around the rocky walls of the remotest limestone gill.

Morning mist obscures Barden far
below in Wharfedale. Earl's Seat and
the summit of Simon's Seat rise out
of the greyness to bring an ethereal
beauty to the scene.

Fantasy to reality

COLIN RAW

The topography of the Yorkshire Dales attracts travellers worldwide who enthuse over its diversity of inspirational scenery. The glacial upheaval during the Ice Age then the appearance of *Homo sapiens* have shaped this unique landscape into something very special. It is here to be treasured.

With dry-stone walls sweeping down the fell-sides to pastured fields below, one is always reminded that this is a working environment. The very foundations of the Dales' attractions have been developed over centuries by the tenacity of farming families taming the land to suit their needs. It is to their credit and pride that we can all enjoy the beauty of this very special area. But with increasing financial constraints plaguing the hill farmers, their numbers are being depleted. They are the real guardians of this landscape. One can only hope that means are made available to preserve this heritage for future generations.

As a photographer there is never any shortage of subject matter in the Dales as I strive to communicate a visual interpretation to any given scene. Throughout the changing seasons the weather orchestrates a variety of moods to create photographic opportunities on a grand scale. Yet to achieve the desired effect often takes lengthy time spans. It is not necessarily a specific scene that offers the ingredients for a pleasing picture, but rather the intriguing lighting situations that develop.

Some visionary expertise is needed to persuade your imagination to project a chosen scene from fantasy to reality. The Dales offer this and more; yet the intricate pre-planning of a shot is always subject to the vagaries of the weather.

To battle against the elements for days and nights at a time, alone on the fells, is indeed an experience to savour. There are days when you curse the wind and rain when the forecasters have promised sunshine; nights when a force eight gale is intent on ripping your frail canvas shelter from some mountain-side; yet through it all you learn a lot about yourself and valuable experience is gained.

The rewards can be awe-inspiring: imagery that other mortals very seldom see; a rising sun at dawn over a mist-filled dale transforms the landscape into a Tolkien fantasy. To experience such grandeur alone is to heighten awareness of the existence of something tangible beyond this earthly span.

Folklore and history are an integral part of the Dales. They give character and meaning, vibrancy to the knowledge as to where the inhabitants come from. Their future as the 21st century looms, is less certain.

From Box Brownie to the sophisticated Bronica medium format camera forty-five years later, Colin Raw now enjoys worldwide publication of his photography. Formerly a textile worker, it was his success in several international photographic contests that finally convinced him of a change of career. Colin, who lives on the edge of the Dales near Skipton, has no cause to regret the decision.

Home ground, where the Farnhill
pinnacle overlooks the Aire Valley.
Rebuilt to commemorate Queen
Victoria's Jubilee.

Raven Scar cairn. Many of these cairns mark the lofty reaches of the Dales and are invaluable when traversing the fells in inclement weather, acting as a much-needed way finder.

A well-preserved limekiln with Ingleborough in the background.

Hardraw Force, Wensleydale,
England's highest waterfall at
ninety-eight feet. The impressive
amphitheatre is visited by thousands
of tourists each year. A small entrance
fee is charged through the Green
Dragon public house.

Majestic Ingleborough shows the
grandeur of the Three Peaks area.
The small tarn with the stillness of
late evening brings tranquillity to the
scene.

Green lanes abound in the Dales.
This one above Stainforth is a typical
example. These were used by the
cattle drovers from as far away as
Scotland.

Spring Crag Wood, near Riddlesden,
resplendent in a carpet of bluebells,
heralds in a much-awaited spring.

Storith Heights farmstead overlooking
Strid Woods at Bolton Abbey on a
haze-shrouded evening.

Dawn mist encroaches upon Barden Moor, the lighting at its most favourable angle of presentation. To witness such grandeur alone is to actually feel the presence of nature at its very best. But you have to set off in the dark to hopefully experience such a spectacle.

A three-day, back-packing trip to Swaledale and Wensleydale was turning into a blank photo shoot. Then miraculously the weather started to change while setting up above Askrigg. If only one decent shot is achieved the journey and effort are not wasted.

A well-preserved hay meadow near Starbotton in Wharfedale. The new Dutch barn may appear as an unwelcome intrusion upon the Dales scene, but the variables of the weather will soon blend it into the landscape.

Buttercup pastures burst forth in June in many parts of the Dales. This one in Birkdale with an old stone barn adds a splash of extra interest to the scene.

J. B. Priestley loved this area of Ribblehead. The subtle late evening light shows Gayle Beck and the old hunting lodge leading the eye to the seemingly flat-topped Simon Fell and Ingleborough.

Addlebrough Hill imposes its flat-topped summit over Askrigg in Wensleydale. The BBC made the village the home base for the *All Creatures Great and Small* series.

DENIS HEALEY'S YORKSHIRE DALES

Nethergill Farm stands amidst the windswept reaches of Oughtershaw. This rough pasture land shows the extremities of grazing that the hill farmers have to face in earning a living from the land.

Muker in Swaledale, another popular
destination. A small craft shop offers
hand-knitted jumpers for sale made
from the wool of local Swaledale sheep,
so helping the economy of these
remote hamlets.

Skipton Church towers up above the older part of the town, the autumn light picking out the colourful details of a wall edging Water Street.

Lovely Gayle in Wensleydale, near Hawes, where the beck tumbles over a series of limestone steps.

You need to get up really early, having
pre-planned the position of the sun,
to capture the warm glow on Bolton
Priory. This was taken at 5.40 am.

Barden Tower, the hunting lodge of Lord Clifford. Autumn pine needles on the road lend extra colour to the scene.

Storm light over Bolton Priory meant a three-hour wait for these conditions to appear. Four visits were made in all, totalling fourteen hours of patience, willing the sun to shine through the squally weather. Not all are sun-kissed days.

FANTASY TO REALITY

An overnight camping stay at Raven
Scar ridge below Ingleborough gave
me superb late evening lighting. The
limestone pavement contrasts well
with the shadowed contours of
Whernside across the valley.

The classic view of Penyghent
overlooking Silverdale. Storm clouds
gathering over the summit emphasise
the ruggedness of the Three Peaks
area.

From the rim of Gordale Scar, Malhamdale, uninterrupted views back to the Craven area of Skipton are possible on a clear day.

The further reaches of Cowside, near Arncliffe. Here an ancient settlement once existed.

This was the site of an ancient settlement above Cowside Beck, near Arncliffe.

Yew Cogar Scar overlooks the twisting Cowside Beck near Arncliffe. This ravine-like offshoot of Littondale is well worth a visit.

Typical of the moorlands around Rylstone when in late August the purple heather stretches into an unending landscape. Grit-stone rockstands abound in this area.

Heathered Deer Gallows plain, at the back of Embsay Moor, has spectacular scenery all round.

DENIS HEALEY'S YORKSHIRE DALES

So many pictures have been taken of Malhamdale that one is constantly on the look out for something new. The grazing sheep and stand of trees highlighted by a late evening sun presented itself near Eshton.

The lone rowan tree adds that extra splash of colour at the very head of Dentdale.

An early morning visit to the River
Ure near Aysgarth captures to best
advantage the contours of the
landscape. The low side lighting picks
out the detail to enhance the beauty of
this part of Wensleydale.

Showers and sunlight are ideal
conditions for photography. This
shot of middle Wharfedale shows
the almost fluorescent greenery of
cultivated fields against the more
sombre looking fell-sides.

DENIS HEALEY'S YORKSHIRE DALES

A storm-lashed day shows the limestone walls sweeping down to the valley bottoms around Langcliffe Scar. Penyghent is a moody monolith on the far skyline.

An autumn evening at Intake pastures,
near Bolton Abbey, gives a warm glow
to this simplistic scene. In ordinary
lighting the impact would be lost.

An early morning start to an autumn
day saw me reach the summit of
Penyghent to capture the last
dispersing streamers of mist from
the colourful flanks.

Embsay Crag and Reservoir, one of
my favourite places. Only half an hour
previously the now-still water was
a cauldron of movement as a savage
wind chilled the bones. Never have
I witnessed the elements change so
swiftly to one of placid peacefulness.

DENIS HEALEY'S YORKSHIRE DALES

Embsay Crag and Reservoir in winter
transform the scene to sparkling
beauty. Even so, a three-hour wait
ensued for a thick cloud covering to
disperse.

Littondale, near Halton Gill, shows
the dark tracery of dry-stone walls
sweeping down the fell-side,
highlighted against the glistening
covering of snow.

Moorgate, Silsden tops, where the isolation of a lone farmstead shows the harsh reality of farming near to the uplands of Rombalds Moor.